CLIENT RETENTION
STRATEGIES
FOR BARBERS

A Comprehensive Guide to Elevating Barbering, Redefining Customer Service Mastery, Building Enduring Client Relationships, Personal Branding and Thriving in the Beauty Industry

WendyCutz G.

Copyright

Disclaimer

The content provided in this book is intended for informational purposes only. While every effort has been made to ensure the accuracy and completeness of the information presented, the author makes no representations or warranties of any kind, express or implied, about the suitability, reliability, or availability of the content for any purpose. The reader acknowledges that the techniques, strategies, and recommendations outlined in this book may not guarantee specific results and should be implemented at their own discretion and risk. The author and publisher shall not be liable for any loss or damage arising from the use of the information contained herein. Readers are advised to seek professional advice and conduct their own research before implementing any practices or techniques discussed in this book.

About The Author

WendyCutz G, a trailblazer in the world of barbering, is not just a skilled professional behind the chair but a visionary redefining the very essence of customer service in this artful industry. With a passion for precision and an eye for detail, WendyCutz G has honed her craft over a few dynamic years in the barber's domain. Her journey isn't just about hair; it's about the transformative power of genuine connections and the art of making every client feel seen, heard, and valued.

In the buzzing world of clippers and shears, WendyCutz G stands out not only for her technical prowess but for her commitment to elevating the client experience. Her approach is a delicate balance between the artistry of barbering and the art of building enduring relationships. A maverick in embracing new trends, WendyCutz G is equally passionate about the human touch in an industry driven by style. As a female barber navigating this traditionally male-dominated field, she brings a unique perspective, challenging norms, and creating a space where everyone is welcome. When WendyCutz G isn't sculpting hairstyles that tell stories, she's on a mission to redefine what it means to be a barber in the 21st century. Her insights, shared in this book, reflect not just professional acumen but a deep understanding of the human connection that makes every snip more than just a cut.

Through this book, she shares the wisdom gained from years behind the chair, offering a roadmap for fellow barbers to transform their craft and build lasting connections. In WendyCutz G's world, barbering isn't just a profession; it's a passion, a canvas for creativity, and a journey of self-discovery. Join her on this expedition to redefine customer service, one cut at a time.

Table of Contents

Introduction

In the dynamic world of barbering, the scissors aren't the only tools shaping success. This book is your guide to unlocking the power of client loyalty and retention, essential pillars for flourishing in the barbering industry.

Picture this—a loyal client, not just a repeat customer, but someone who eagerly anticipates their next visit. Client loyalty goes beyond a transaction; it's a connection that transforms a haircut into an experience. The significance of cultivating loyal clientele extends far beyond the confines of your barbershop; it's the heartbeat of sustained success. Yet, navigating the path to client loyalty isn't without its challenges. In an industry that's both personal and competitive, understanding the nuances of client retention becomes paramount. This book delves into the intricacies of building lasting connections, turning challenges into opportunities for growth.

As a barber, you're not just a sculptor of hair; you're an architect of relationships. Let us explore the why, how, and what of client loyalty, discovering the transformative impact it can have on your craft and your business. Get ready to embark on a journey where each page holds insights, strategies, and practical tips to elevate your barber-client relationships to new heights.

Your success story starts now!

Chapter 1
UNDERSTANDING CLIENT BEHAVIOR

Client loyalty is not merely a transactional outcome; it's deeply rooted in the psychological dynamics between the barber and the client. By unraveling the intricacies of client decision-making, we can uncover the keys to fostering lasting connections.

Trust

At the core of client loyalty lies trust. Clients seek a barber they can rely on, not just for a great haircut but for an experience built on trust. Establishing trust involves consistency, reliability, and a genuine commitment to meeting and exceeding client expectations.

Personal Connection

As a female barber, my experience has taught me that beyond the haircut itself, clients crave a personal connection. Understanding a client's preferences, remembering details about their life, and engaging in meaningful conversations contribute to a sense of belonging. This personal touch transforms a routine appointment into a cherished experience.

Perceived Value

Clients assess the value they receive from a barber beyond the monetary exchange. The overall experience, including the ambiance of the shop, the quality of service, and the attention to detail, shapes the perceived value. Demonstrating that the service goes above and beyond expectations is a key influencer.

Emotional Engagement

Human emotions play a significant role in client loyalty. Positive emotions associated with a barber, the shop, and the experience create a powerful bond. Conversely, negative emotions can lead to dissatisfaction and, ultimately, client attrition. Understanding and managing these emotional connections are crucial.

Consistency and Reliability

Consistency builds trust, and reliability fosters dependability. Clients appreciate a barber who consistently delivers high-quality service, maintains a welcoming atmosphere, and is reliable in meeting scheduled appointments. Inconsistencies can erode trust and jeopardize client loyalty.

Brand Image and Reputation

The perception of a barber's brand and reputation greatly influences client decisions. Positive reviews, word-of-mouth recommendations, and a strong online presence contribute to building a reputable image. Clients often choose barbers based on the perceived reputation of the shop and the skills of the barber.

Understanding these psychological factors provides the foundation for effective client retention strategies.

In the following chapters, we'll delve into actionable steps to leverage these insights, ensuring a positive and enduring connection with clients.

Chapter 2

WHY SHOULD CLIENTS BE LOYAL TO YOU

The concept of loyalty, in the vibrant tapestry of the barbering world, is a two-way street. As barbers, you hold the key to crafting a unique value proposition that not only keeps clients coming back but also makes them enthusiastic advocates for your craft. You should bear in mind that different clients would keep coming to you for different reasons.

Some of the reasons why clients would remain loyal to you include

Craftsmanship and Expertise
At the heart of your value proposition is your craftsmanship. Clients seek not just a haircut but an artful transformation. Your expertise, precision, and ability to bring their vision to life set you apart. By consistently delivering

exceptional results, you create a compelling reason for clients to stay loyal.

Personalized Experiences

Every client is unique, and recognizing and celebrating this individuality contributes to a personalized experience. Whether it's remembering their preferred style or engaging in genuine conversations, personalized interactions build a bond that extends beyond the chair. Clients appreciate the effort to make each visit special.

Trust and Reliability

Building trust goes hand in hand with client loyalty. Being a reliable and trustworthy barber establishes a foundation for a long-term relationship. Clients should feel confident that each visit will meet or exceed their expectations, fostering a sense of security and satisfaction.

Comprehensive Care and Recommendations

Going beyond the haircut by offering comprehensive care. Providing grooming tips, recommendations is a holistic approach that elevates the client experience and solidifies your value proposition. This will be discussed in detail later on.

Chapter 3

EVERYONE IS A POTENTIAL CLIENT

In the realm of barbering, every interaction is not just a haircut; it's a gateway to untapped business potential. Every moment in the barber's chair is an opportunity for growth. Consider each client not only as someone seeking a service but as a potential ambassador for your brand.

- Engage in genuine conversations, actively listen, and leave a lasting impression. Satisfied clients are more likely to recommend your services, leading to organic growth.

- Harness the power of word-of-mouth marketing. A satisfied client is a walking advertisement. Encourage clients to share their positive experiences with friends and family. A personal recommendation can be one of the most effective ways to attract new clients.

- Consider incentivizing your existing clients to refer others by implementing a referral program. Offer discounts, complimentary services, or exclusive perks for every successful referral. This not only expands your client base but also rewards those who contribute to your business growth.

- Become an active participant in your community. Sponsor local events, collaborate with neighboring businesses, or participate in community gatherings. Establishing a visible presence can make your barbershop a go-to destination for locals.

- Create buzz around your barbershop by hosting special promotions or events. This could include themed haircut days, exclusive discounts, or collaborative events with local influencers. These initiatives not only attract attention but also foster a sense of community around your brand.

- Explore collaborations with other businesses in your area. Partnering with local salons, clothing stores, or even cafes can open up new avenues for client outreach. Cross-promotions can introduce your services to a broader audience.

By recognizing the business potential in every interaction and implementing strategic outreach methods, you not only expand your client base but also position your barbershop as a dynamic and growing establishment within the community.

Chapter 4

EVERYBODY IS SOMEBODY

It is very crucial to understand that every individual who steps into your chair is not just a client; they are somebody with unique preferences, stories, and expectations; so you must be intentional about weaving a tapestry of lasting impressions that keep clients returning, knowing they will always be treated as somebody special.

Below are some tips that can help you

Personalized Consultations

Begin each session with a personalized consultation. Take the time to understand the client's preferences, lifestyle, and desired style. This not only enhances the quality of the haircut but also establishes a connection, making the experience more personal.

Attentive Listening

Being an attentive listener is a skill that elevates the client experience. Pay close attention to their preferences, concerns, and any specific requests. Engaging in meaningful conversations builds rapport and makes the client feel valued.

Detailed and Thorough Services

Excellence in service extends beyond the haircut. Pay meticulous attention to detail, ensuring a thorough and comprehensive service. From precise cutting techniques to meticulous grooming, each element contributes to a memorable overall experience.

Comfort and Relaxation

Create an environment that promotes comfort and relaxation. Utilize comfortable chairs, provide neck and shoulder massages, and use soothing scents. A relaxed client is more likely to enjoy the experience and return for future appointments.

Thoughtful Extras

Incorporate thoughtful extras into the service. Offer a hot towel treatment, provide complimentary grooming products, or even a post-haircut styling session. These additional touches go a long way in making the experience special.

Engaging Conversations

While maintaining professionalism, engage in conversations that go beyond the haircut. Learn about your clients' interests, milestones, and experiences. Building a personal connection fosters a sense of camaraderie and ensures a memorable visit.

Showcase Expertise and Creativity

Demonstrate your expertise and creativity throughout the service. Whether it's suggesting a new style, recommending grooming techniques, or showcasing your artistic flair, clients appreciate barbers who take pride in their craft.

Personalized Post-Service Recommendations

After completing the service, provide personalized recommendations for at-home care and styling. Offering insights on maintaining the haircut reinforces your commitment to the client's ongoing satisfaction.

Create a Personalized Experience

Tailor each visit to the client's preferences. Remember details such as preferred styling products, preferred length, or specific techniques they favor. This level of personalization shows that you value their individuality.

Chapter 5

CREATING A
RECIPROCAL BOND

Prioritizing a warm and friendly environment serves as the ballroom and understanding the reciprocal nature of client relationships not only enhance the overall client experience but also create a positive cycle where clients feel compelled to return and share their positive experiences with others. Let's unravel the importance of cultivating an inviting space where the client feels not just seen, but genuinely welcomed.

Creating a Haven of Comfort

The moment a client steps into your barbershop, they should feel a sense of comfort and ease. From the ambiance to the decor, every element should contribute to a welcoming atmosphere. A comfortable client is more likely to engage and return.

Personalized Greetings and Recognition

The first impression sets the tone. Greet clients by name, remembering details from previous visits. This personal touch communicates that each client is not just a customer but a valued individual. Recognition fosters a sense of belonging and familiarity.

Open Communication and Friendliness

Encourage open communication and cultivate a friendly demeanor. A warm conversation can turn a routine visit into a memorable experience. Clients appreciate barbers who are approachable, willing to listen, and create a space where they feel heard.

Thoughtful Waiting Areas

The waiting area is a crucial part of the overall experience. Ensure it is comfortable, well-lit, and equipped with engaging material. Thoughtful waiting areas contribute to a positive pre-service experience and showcase your commitment to client well-being.

Attentive Service

Beyond technical skills, attentiveness is a cornerstone of a welcoming environment. Anticipate client needs, offer refreshments, and ensure their comfort throughout the service. Small gestures go a long way in creating a positive and reciprocal relationship.

Inclusive and Diverse Representation

A welcoming atmosphere embraces diversity. Ensure your barbershop is inclusive and representative of different backgrounds. Clients appreciate environments that celebrate diversity and make everyone feel accepted; this includes things like the kind of music you play.

Cleanliness and Organization

A clean and organized space contributes to a sense of professionalism and care. Clients value a tidy environment, and it reflects your commitment to providing a high-quality experience.

Chapter 6

PERSONALIZE EVERY SERVICE

As previously mentioned, personalization is the key to unlocking enduring client relationships and building trust. To make every haircut a unique journey and enhance the overall client experience:

- Initiate and engage in meaningful conversations with your clients. Beyond discussing haircut preferences, delve into their interests, hobbies, and daily life. Actively listen to their stories, as these conversations provide valuable insights into their preferences.

- Create client profiles or maintain notes for each individual. Record details such as preferred haircut styles, grooming product preferences, and any specific likes or dislikes. Referencing these notes during subsequent visits showcases your commitment to personalization.

- Utilize questionnaires or surveys to gather information about clients' preferences. This structured approach allows you to understand their expectations, preferred grooming routines, and any specific concerns they might have.

- Conduct consistent client consultations before each service. Ask about any changes in preferences, explore new styles, and ensure you are aligned with their expectations. This ongoing dialogue fosters open communication and reinforces the personalization of the experience.

- Offer personalized grooming recommendations based on individual hair types, face shapes, and styling preferences. Educate clients on suitable products and techniques to maintain their haircut between visits. This guidance adds value to the service and enhances the client's grooming routine.

- During the haircut, provide thoughtful suggestions for styling or grooming adjustments. This could include recommending a slight alteration to the length, trying a new styling product, or exploring variations of their chosen style. These suggestions showcase your expertise and dedication to their satisfaction.

- Take note of clients' milestones and special occasions, such as birthdays or anniversaries. Acknowledge and celebrate these moments with personalized gesturcs, whether it's a complimentary service or a small token of appreciation. Such thoughtful actions strengthen the emotional connection

- After the service, engage in follow-up communications. Send personalized messages expressing gratitude for their visit and inquire about their satisfaction. This post-service interaction reinforces the personalized touch and demonstrates your commitment to their well-being.

- Actively seek and respond to client feedback. Use their input to make adjustments and refinements to future services. This iterative process ensures that each experience is a continuous improvement tailored to their evolving preferences.

Chapter 7

IDENTITY AND CELEBRATE LOYAL CUSTOMERS

Acknowledging and honoring loyal clientele forms the foundation of lasting connections. This chapter delves into the significance of recognizing and appreciating the clients who choose your barbershop consistently. Additionally, we'll explore creative ways to offer special deals and the pivotal role promotions play in retaining these valued clients.

Some of the ways to honor and celebrate loyal clients include:

Personalized Loyalty Programs Develop personalized loyalty programs that cater to individual preferences. Offer exclusive perks, such as discounted services, priority scheduling, or complementary grooming products. Tailoring loyalty rewards enhances the sense of appreciation for each client's unique loyalty journey.

Tiered Loyalty Systems

Implement tiered loyalty systems where clients can progress to higher levels based on the frequency of their visits or accumulated points. Each tier can unlock progressively valuable rewards, creating a gamified and engaging loyalty experience.

Special Occasion Recognition

Recognize special occasions in the lives of loyal clients, such as anniversaries of their first visit to your barbershop. Consider offering special deals or personalized gifts during these milestones, creating a sense of celebration and appreciation.

VIP Treatment Days

Designate specific days or hours for VIP treatment exclusively for loyal clients. This could involve additional pampering services, complimentary refreshments, or priority access. The exclusivity of these moments enhances the client's feeling of being valued.

Birthday Bonus

Celebrate clients' birthdays with personalized bonuses. Offer special deals, discounts, or complementary services during their birthday month. This thoughtful gesture not only acknowledges their loyalty but also adds a personal touch to the relationship.

Referral Recognition Programs

Encourage loyal clients to become advocates for your barbershop through referral recognition programs. Acknowledge and reward clients who refer new customers, showcasing gratitude for their role in expanding your clientele.

Limited-Time Loyalty Promotions

Periodically introducc limited-time promotions exclusively for loyal clients. This could involve discounted rates on specific services, bundled packages, or buy-one-get-one deals. Creating a sense of urgency adds excitement to these promotions.

Client Appreciation Events

Host client appreciation events to celebrate the collective loyalty of your clientele. This could be a social gathering, a themed day at the barbershop, or even exclusive access to new services. These events foster a sense of community among your loyal clients.

Loyalty-Driven Collaborations

Explore collaborations with other businesses to provide unique benefits to loyal clients. Partnering with local establishments for cross-promotions introduces clients to a broader range of experiences and further enhances their loyalty.

The importance of acknowledging and honoring loyal clientele goes beyond transactional interactions. It's about fostering a sense of belonging, recognition, and appreciation. By incorporating creative and personalized approaches to loyalty programs and promotions, you not only retain clients but also deepen the emotional connection, making them not just customers but cherished members of your barbershop community.

Chapter 8

COMMUNICATION STRATEGIES

Open communication creates a bridge between barbers and clients, fostering understanding and trust. It is the key to preempting misunderstandings, addressing concerns promptly, and building lasting connections.

Here are some tips to foster openness and address concerns.

- Create an environment that encourages open communication. Ensure your barbershop atmosphere is welcoming, and clients feel at ease expressing their thoughts and concerns. A relaxed setting promotes candid conversations.

- Practice active listening during consultations and throughout the service.

Demonstrate genuine interest in what clients are saying, and paraphrase to confirm understanding. This not only enhances the client experience but also signals that their input is valued.

- Actively encourage clients to provide feedback on their experiences. Display signage or verbally express that you welcome suggestions, concerns, or compliments. An open invitation for feedback helps you address issues proactively.

- Incorporate timely check-ins during the service. Ask if clients are comfortable with the length, style, or any specific aspects of the haircut. This real-time feedback allows you to make adjustments and ensures client satisfaction.

- When addressing concerns, use tactful questioning to gather more information. Instead of asking accusatory questions, frame inquiries in a way that invites constructive dialogue. This approach helps clients express concerns without feeling defensive.

- Respond to concerns with empathy. Acknowledge the client's feelings and express understanding. This empathetic approach demonstrates that you prioritize their satisfaction and are committed to finding solutions.

- Propose practical solutions to address concerns. Whether it's a misunderstanding about the desired style or a specific grooming preference, collaboratively explore alternatives that align with the client's expectations.

- Establish follow-up procedures to ensure that addressed concerns have been resolved to the client's satisfaction. This commitment to follow-through demonstrates accountability and reinforces your dedication to client well-being.

- Use client feedback as a catalyst for continuous improvement. Regularly assess and refine your services based on the insights gained from communication. Clients appreciate businesses that actively seek to enhance the customer experience.

Chapter 9

USE FEEDBACK TO REFINE CUSTOMER EXPERIENCE

Continuous improvement isn't just a philosophy; it's a strategic necessity for any thriving business. It showcases adaptability, responsiveness to client needs, and a commitment to providing an ever-enhancing experience. Embrace client input as a guiding compass, steering your barbershop towards a future of excellence and enduring client loyalty.

Below are effective ways to collect and utilize client feedback

Anonymous Feedback Channels

Create anonymous channels for clients to provide feedback. Whether through suggestion boxes, online surveys, or digital forms, offering anonymity encourages honest and candid responses, providing unfiltered insights.

Post-Service Surveys
Implement post-service surveys to gather specific feedback on the client's experience. Tailor questions to assess various aspects such as service quality, communication, and overall satisfaction. Consistent use of surveys creates a structured feedback loop.

Personalized Follow-Up Emails
Send personalized follow-up emails after client visits, expressing gratitude and requesting feedback. This one-on-one approach shows genuine interest in the client's perspective and provides an opportunity for them to share detailed insights.

Social Media Polls and Q&A Sessions
Leverage social media platforms to conduct polls and Q&A sessions. Engaging clients through these interactive channels not only gathers feedback but also strengthens the online community around your barbershop.

In-Shop Feedback Stations

Set up physical feedback stations within the barbershop. Equip these stations with simple forms or tablets where clients can share their thoughts immediately after their service. This real-time approach captures instant impressions.

Encouraging Verbal Feedback

During and after services, actively encourage clients to share verbal feedback. Create an atmosphere where clients feel comfortable expressing their thoughts openly. Verbal communication can unveil nuances that written feedback might miss.

Feedback Incentives

Incentivize feedback participation by offering discounts, exclusive promotions, or entry into loyalty programs. Clients are more likely to provide feedback when they perceive a tangible benefit, contributing to a mutually beneficial relationship.

Regular Team Feedback Sessions

Foster a culture of continuous improvement within the barbering team. Conduct regular feedback sessions where barbers collectively discuss client input, share best practices, and collaboratively work towards refining services.

Analyzing Patterns and Trends

Systematically analyze patterns and trends within client feedback. Look for recurring themes or common areas of improvement. Identifying these trends allows barbers to address systemic issues and prioritize areas for enhancement.

Implementing Actionable Changes

Most importantly, act upon the feedback received. Implement actionable changes based on client input. Whether it's refining service protocols, adjusting communication practices, or introducing new amenities, tangible improvements demonstrate a commitment to client satisfaction.

Chapter 10

APPOINTMENT MANAGEMENT

Mastering the art of appointment management can help barbers and barbershops shops to streamline operations and also enhance the overall client experience. Efficient scheduling fosters a sense of professionalism, ensures client satisfaction, and optimizes revenue generation—a win-win for both barbers and their clientele.

This chapter explores the crucial significance of streamlined scheduling and presents effective strategies to minimize no-shows while maximizing the number of appointments, ensuring optimal utilization of your time and resources.

Online Appointment Systems

Implement user-friendly online appointment systems that allow clients to schedule, reschedule, or cancel appointments with ease. This convenience not only attracts tech-savvy clients but also reduces the likelihood of no-shows as they can manage their bookings effortlessly.

Appointment Reminders

Send automated appointment reminders via SMS, email, or mobile apps. Reminders serve as a gentle nudge for clients, reducing the chances of forgetfulness and minimizing no-shows. Include essential details such as date, time, and any pre-appointment instructions.

Confirmation Calls

Consider implementing confirmation calls for high-value or long-duration appointments. A personal touch through a brief call reinforces the commitment, provides an opportunity to address any queries, and ensures both parties are on the same page.

Flexible Cancellation Policies

Establish clear and fair cancellation policies. While flexibility is crucial, setting guidelines for advance notice for cancellations or rescheduling helps minimize last-minute disruptions and encourages clients to respect their appointments.

Overbooking Strategies

Implement strategic overbooking for peak hours, where the likelihood of no-shows is higher. Use historical data to identify patterns and adjust the schedule to accommodate a slight overbooking without compromising service quality.

Incentivize Timely Arrivals

Incentivize clients to arrive on time by offering discounts, promotions, or loyalty points for punctuality. Communicate the importance of being on time to ensure a smooth and efficient experience for both the client and the barber.

Waitlist Management

Efficiently manage waitlists for fully booked time slots. Notify clients on the waitlist of any available openings due to cancellations, giving them the opportunity to secure a last-minute appointment.

Monitoring and Analytics

Regularly monitor appointment data and utilize analytics to identify trends, peak hours, and areas for improvement. This data-driven approach allows for continuous refinement of scheduling strategies based on the unique dynamics of your barbershop.

Chapter 11

UNDER PROMISE AND OVER DELIVER

Excellence in service is the heartbeat of a successful barbering career. In this chapter, we delve into the essential elements of delivering outstanding service in the context of barbering, emphasizing the pivotal importance of setting and consistently exceeding service standards.

Precision and Craftsmanship

- Setting Standards: Define precise cutting techniques, grooming standards, and attention to detail that reflect the level of craftsmanship expected in your barbershop

- Exceeding Standards: Consistently deliver haircuts and grooming services with impeccable precision, showcasing mastery in your craft that goes beyond client expectations.

Welcoming Atmosphere

- Setting Standards: Establish a warm and inviting ambiance within the barbershop, ensuring clients feel comfortable and welcomed from the moment they walk in.

- Exceeding Standards: Go the extra mile to create a personalized and memorable atmosphere, making each client feel like a valued part of the barbershop community.

Communication and Consultation

- Setting Standards: Establish clear communication protocols, emphasizing active listening during consultations to understand clients' preferences and expectations.

- Exceeding Standards: Engage in meaningful conversations, providing expert advice and personalized recommendations. Ensure clients leave not just with a great haircut but also with insights into grooming and styling.

Time Management

- Setting Standards: Set realistic appointment durations, ensuring punctuality and efficiency in service delivery.

- Exceeding Standards: Strive to complete services with optimal speed without compromising quality. Surprise clients with a seamless experience that respects their time commitments.

Grooming Recommendations

- Setting Standards: Offer basic grooming tips and product recommendations as part of the service.

- Exceeding Standards: Provide in-depth grooming guidance, offering insights into at-home care routines, styling techniques, and personalized product recommendations tailored to each client's needs.

Professionalism and Hygiene

- Setting Standards: Establish high standards of professionalism, emphasizing hygiene and maintaining a clean and organized workspace.

- Exceeding Standards: Exemplify impeccable professionalism by exceeding hygiene norms, presenting a well-groomed appearance, and ensuring the barbershop environment reflects a commitment to excellence.

Client Education

- Setting Standards: Share basic information about haircut styles and grooming procedures during consultations.

- Exceeding Standards: Actively educate clients on current trends, styling options, and the artistry behind the services. Foster a culture of client empowerment by enhancing their understanding of grooming practices.

Personalization and Recognition

- Setting Standards: Implement a system for recording client preferences and details for a personalized experience.

- Exceeding Standards: Go beyond basic personalization by actively remembering and celebrating client milestones, preferences, and special occasions. Demonstrate a level of recognition that transcends the ordinary.

Problem Resolution

- Setting Standards: Establish a protocol for addressing client concerns and resolving issues in a timely and professional manner.

- Exceeding Standards: Proactively anticipate potential concerns, and go the extra mile to resolve issues with genuine concern and a commitment to exceeding client expectations.

Continuous Improvement

- Setting Standards: Emphasize the importance of continuous improvement in service delivery through regular training and feedback loops.

- Exceeding Standards: Instill a culture of constant growth and refinement. Actively seek client feedback, analyze trends, and implement innovative strategies to elevate the overall service experience continually.

Chapter 12

SOCIAL MEDIA AND MARKETING

The impact of social media in the dynamic landscape of the barbering industry is profound, shaping trends, influencing client decisions, and providing an avenue for business growth. Social media is not just a promotional tool; it's a dynamic platform that shapes perceptions and fosters connections.

Let us explore the significance of harnessing the potential of social media for your barbering career

Community Engagement
Social media platforms create virtual communities where barbers can engage with existing clients and attract new ones. Fosters a sense of community by sharing behind-the-scenes glimpses, client

transformations, and interactive content. Encourage clients to share their experiences and engage in conversations.

Trend Showcase

Social media is a visual medium, making it ideal for showcasing haircut trends, grooming styles, and the artistry of barbering. Regularly post high-quality images and videos of your work. Keep up with industry trends and incorporate them into your content to position your barbershop as a trendsetter.

Client Testimonials and Reviews

Positive client testimonials and reviews on social media serve as powerful endorsements, influencing potential clients. Encourage clients to share their experiences on platforms like Google, Facebook, or Instagram. Feature these testimonials in your social media content to build trust and credibility.

Brand Personality

You can showcase your brand personality, values, and unique offerings on social media by developing a consistent brand voice and visual identity. Share content that reflects the personality of your barbershop, whether it's professionalism, creativity, or a blend of both.

Promotions and Specials

Social media is an effective means for promoting special deals, discounts, and exclusive offers. Create visually appealing promotional content. Utilize Instagram and Facebook ads to target specific demographics and maximize the reach of your promotions.

Educational Content

With social media, you can shat educational content about grooming tips, styling techniques, and product recommendations. Establish your barbershop as an authority in the field by offering valuable insights that benefit your audience.

Influencer Collaborations

Collaborating with influencers in the beauty and grooming niche can amplify your barbershop's reach and credibility. Identify local influencers or those with a significant following in your target market. Offer them complimentary services in exchange for social media coverage and reviews.

Real-Time Updates

Social media enables real-time updates, keeping clients informed about promotions, schedule changes, or special events. Regularly update your social media platforms with current information. Utilize Instagram Stories, Facebook posts, or Twitter updates to share timely announcements.

Visual Consistency

Maintaining visual consistency across social media platforms enhances brand recognition and professionalism. Use consistent color schemes, fonts, and imagery. Create a visually cohesive feed that reflects the aesthetic of your barbershop.

Analytics and Insights

Analyzing social media metrics provides valuable insights into audience engagement, content performance, and overall impact. Utilize analytics tools on platforms like Instagram and Facebook to understand your audience demographics, peak engagement times, and the effectiveness of your content strategy.

Here's a guide on how to analyze social media metrics

Reach and Impression: Reach represents the total number of unique users who have seen your content, while impressions indicate the total number of times your content has been displayed.

- What to you: Assess the overall visibility of your content and identify popular posts. A higher reach may indicate effective audience targeting.

Engagement Rates: Engagement rate is the percentage of people who interact with your content (likes, comments, shares) relative to the total number of impressions.

- What to do: Evaluate the level of audience engagement. High engagement rates suggest that your content resonates with your audience, contributing to community building.

Follower Growth: Track the growth or decline in your follower count over time.

- What to do: Understand the impact of your content strategy on attracting and retaining followers. Consistent growth indicates a healthy and engaged audience.

Click-Through Rates (CTR):
CTR measures the percentage of users who clicked on a link in your post compared to the total number of users who viewed the post.

- What to do: Evaluate the effectiveness of call-to-action elements in your posts. A higher CTR indicates that your audience is interested in taking the next step.

Demographic Insights: Platforms often provide demographic information about your audience, including age, gender, location, and interests.

- What to do: Tailor your content and engagement strategies based on the demographics of your audience. Understand who engages the most and create content that resonates with them.

Top-Performing Content: Identify which types of content (images, videos, stories) and topics resonate the most with your audience.

- What to do: Optimize your content strategy by focusing on the types of posts that generate the most engagement. Adjust your content calendar based on these insights.

Hashtag Performance: Evaluate the effectiveness of hashtags used in your posts.

- What to do: Determine which hashtags drive the most engagement and reach. Incorporate trending and relevant hashtags to increase the discoverability of your content.

Post Timing: Analyze the times and days when your posts receive the highest engagement.

- What to do: Optimize your posting schedule to reach your audience when they are most active. This helps increase visibility and engagement.

Sentiment Analysis: Assess the sentiment of comments and mentions (positive, negative, neutral).

- What to do: Understand how your audience perceives your brand. Address any negative sentiments promptly and leverage positive feedback in your marketing.

Conversion Tracking: Track the number of users who take a desired action, such as booking appointments through a link in your social media posts.

- What to do: Measure the effectiveness of your social media in converting followers into clients. Adjust your strategies based on the conversion data.

Case Study 1

Shop Name: Perfect Touch Barbershop
Strategy: The Personal Touch

Perfect Touch Barbershop, a traditional neighborhood barbershop, faced the challenge of retaining clients in a competitive market where newer, trendier establishments were emerging.

Approach Employed

a. Personalized Client Profiles: Perfect Touch Barbershop implemented a system to create personalized client profiles, including haircut preferences, grooming product choices, and relevant personal details.

b. Birthday Bonuses: The shop started offering personalized discounted service during the client's birthday month.

c. Recognition and Conversations: The barbers were trained to actively engaged in conversations. Recognition became a cornerstone of their service.

d. Referral Rewards: Perfect Touch Barbershop introduced a referral program where existing clients received discounts for referring new clients to the shop.

OUTCOME

Clients at Perfect Touch Barbershop felt a strong sense of connection and recognition. The personalized approach and thoughtful gestures, such as birthday bonuses, created a loyal customer base. The referral program not only attracted new clients but also strengthened the sense of community within the shop.

Case Study 2

**Shop Name: The Place Grooming Lounge
Strategy: Digital Engagement**

The Place Grooming Lounge, a modern barbershop in a bustling urban setting, aimed to enhance client retention by leveraging digital platforms.

Approach Employed

a. Online Booking and Reminders: They implemented an online booking system with automated reminders, making it convenient for clients to schedule appointments and reducing no-shows.

b. Social Media Engagement: The shop actively used Instagram and Facebook to showcase the barbers' skills, share grooming tips, and engage with clients through polls, Q&A sessions, and client features.

c. Exclusive Promotions: The Place Grooming Lounge ran exclusive promotions and discounts for social media followers, encouraging clients to follow and engage with the barbershop's online presence.

d. Client Spotlights: They started sharing before-and-after photos along with personal stories. This not only showcased the barbers' work but also highlighted the diverse clientele.

OUTCOME

The implementation of digital strategies significantly improved appointment management, reduced no-shows, and attracted a broader online audience. The Place Grooming Lounge developed a vibrant online community, with engaged followers who felt connected to the barbershop's brand and services.

These case studies demonstrate that successful client retention strategies go beyond the haircut. Personalization, recognition, digital engagement, and community-building are integral components that contribute to the long-term success of barbershops in a competitive market.

Conclusion

In the pages of this book, we've embarked on a journey to transform the art of barbering into a profound experience, one that extends beyond the shear and clipper. As barbers, you hold the power not just to shape hair but to craft lasting connections, foster loyalty, and cultivate a thriving community around your barbershop.

From the significance of personalized client experiences to the strategic utilization of social media, each chapter has been a guide to elevate your approach. The essence lies in understanding that client retention is not merely a transactional exchange; it's an ongoing relationship built on trust, recognition, and a commitment to excellence.

As you implement the discussed strategies, remember that your impact goes beyond the haircut. It's in the meticulous attention to detail, the warmth of a welcoming atmosphere, and the seamless scheduling that respects your clients' time. It's in the community you build online, showcasing your artistry, and fostering engagement that extends beyond the physical walls of your barbershop.

The success of your journey lies in continuous improvement, in the adaptability to new trends, and in the genuine desire to exceed service standards. By embracing the personal touch, harnessing technology, and creating a strong online presence, you not only retain clients but shape a brand that stands resilient in the ever-evolving world of grooming.

So, as you step back into your barbershop armed with insights, remember that each client in your chair is more than just a haircut; they are a canvas waiting to be transformed, a story waiting to be heard. Nurturing these connections is not just a business strategy; it's an art, and you, dear barbers, are the artists shaping excellence, one client at a time. May your scissors be sharp, your clippers be precise, and your relationships be enduring. Here's to the artistry of barbering and the flourishing journey that lies ahead.

www.ingramcontent.com/pod-product-compliance
Lightning Source LLC
Chambersburg PA
CBHW072255310526
45795CB00012B/1660